THE
UNOFFICIAL
GUIDE TO CRAFTING
THE WORLD OF
Harry Potter

30 Magical Crafts for Witches and Wizards—from
Pencil Wands to House Colors Tie-Dye Shirts

JAMIE HARRINGTON

Foreword by Dinah Bucholz, *New York Times* **Bestselling Author of** *The Unofficial Harry Potter Cookbook*

Adamsmedia
Avon, Massachusetts

Published by

Adams Media, a division of F+W Media, Inc.

57 Littlefield Street, Avon, MA 02322. U.S.A.

www.adamsmedia.com

ISBN 10: 1-4405-9504-6

ISBN 13: 978-1-4405-9504-2

eISBN 10: 1-4405-9505-4

eISBN 13: 978-1-4405-9505-9

Printed by RR Donnelley, Harrisonburg, VA, U.S.A.

10   9   8   7   6   5   4   3   2

September 2016

Library of Congress Cataloging-in-Publication Data

Harrington, Jamie, author.

The unofficial guide to crafting the world of Harry Potter

/ Jamie Harrington.

Avon, Massachusetts: Adams Media [2016]

Includes index.

LCCN 2016003925 (print) | LCCN 2016014572 (ebook) | ISBN

9781440595042 (pb) | ISBN 1440595046 (pb) | ISBN 9781440595059 (ebook) | ISBN 1440595054 (ebook)

LCSH: Handicraft--Juvenile literature. | Rowling, J.K.--Themes,

 motives--Juvenile literature. | Potter, Harry (Fictitious

 character)--Juvenile literature.

LCC TT160 .H358 2016 (print) | LCC TT160 (ebook) | DDC

 745.5--dc23

LC record available at *http://lccn.loc.gov/2016003925*

Cover design by Sylvia McArdle.

Cover images by F+W Media, Inc.

Interior images by iStockphoto.com and F+W Media, Inc.

This book is available at quantity discounts for bulk purchases.

For information, please call 1-800-289-0963.

DEDICATION

For Halle. The coolest Mudblood I know.
Consider this your Hogwarts letter.

CONTENTS

FOREWORD

What should we Harry Potter–obsessed, well, Potterheads do in between Potter-themed book and movie releases? What to do with our twiddly thumbs? Jamie Harrington provides the perfect solution to this pesky problem in this book on crafting your way into Harry Potter's world. It would be almost worth it for me to go back to school—almost, because, frankly, who misses homework and droning teachers?—to turn an ordinary school composition notebook into a spellbook.

But there are plenty of crafts for young and old alike.

The projects in these pages are not only super cool but also gorgeous. Bring holiday cheer to your Slytherin common room with a Snake Door Wreath that evokes the beauty of ancient Greek carvings of Medusa. Ponder your deepest desire while shaving, brushing your teeth, or applying makeup before an antique Mirror of Erised, and fall asleep each night to the vision of hauntingly spectral Floating Candle Night Lights. Flaunt your house colors with your own hand-dyed shirt and welcome friends into your home with a House Banners Doormat to truly feel like you are inhabiting the world of Hogwarts.

We Potterheads love to feel like we are living inside the Harry Potter books, and there is nothing like eating the food the characters eat and decorating our surroundings with objects like the crafts in these pages that brings this magical world into our lives.

—DINAH BUCHOLZ, *New York Times* Bestselling Author of
The Unofficial Harry Potter Cookbook

INTRODUCTION

Wands and magic spells. Pensieves and Remembralls. House-elves and monsters.

Who doesn't love the world of Harry Potter and all the adventure and mystery that come along with it? Now, with *The Unofficial Guide to Crafting the World of Harry Potter* you can bring a little bit of that magic into your bedroom, locker, and even your own backyard!

Here you'll find thirty magic-filled crafts that are simple enough to do even if you're a beginner, but cool enough that you'll have fun making them even as an advanced crafter. So many of these projects can be made with things you have around your house already like sugar or toothpicks, and with just an afternoon of free time. This isn't just a book where your parents or other grownups get to do all the crafting while you watch! Whatever your age, you're guaranteed to find lots of different activities you can either do entirely on your own, like the Sugar Quill Headband and Mad-Eye Moody Photo Frame, or with just a little help, like the Mandrake Root Pencil Holder and the Dementor Soap. You'll find some crafts in the book that use materials like spray paint or a hot glue gun. Be sure to check in with an adult before using these items, and for the hot glue gun, I recommend using a cool-temperature glue gun to help keep you safe.

I have spent countless hours crafting and writing about my love for all things nerd at my blog, *Totally The Bomb* (www.totallythebomb.com), but putting all my favorite Harry Potter crafts together in one place for you is the most fun I have had so far. When I was a camp counselor, I snuck the Harry Potter books off the campers' bedside tables while they were asleep, and when my daughter Halle (or as she's known on YouTube, Hallecake; you can find her channel here: *http://youtube.com/Hallecake*) was old enough to read the series herself, I got to experience the magic again through her eyes. These Harry Potter–inspired crafts give us something in common, and when we laugh over what flavors to include in our Every Flavor Beans or argue over the perfect shade of Gryffindor yellow, it means I get to spend the entire afternoon with my daughter, and that's what I love the most. Halle and I both picked out our favorites to share with you. She's the expert in our house when it comes to all things Harry Potter so I bow to her knowledge, and she personally assured me that each and every craft in here—from the Spellbook Journal to the Butterbeer Lip Balm to the Floating Candle Night Lights—will blow you away.

Whether you're looking for something totally Potter-tastic to wear, to help you organize your desk, or to personalize your bedroom, you can easily find something to create no matter what kind of mood you're in. *Accio* crafting materials! Let's do this.

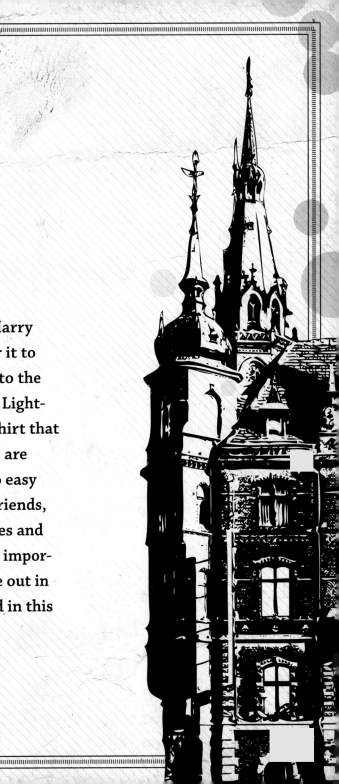

CHAPTER 1

THE SCHOOL TRUNK: CRAFTS TO WEAR

In our house, we are huge fans of showing our Harry Potter love with the things we wear. We like for it to be a little simple—something that doesn't shout to the whole world you're wearing Potter gear—like the Lightning Scar Earrings or the House Colors Tie-Dye Shirt that might make people do a double-take. These crafts are a lot of fun to make for yourself, but they are also easy enough that you can make a few extras for your friends, too. After all, it's important to pack the right robes and uniform attire in your school trunk—just like it's important to have a full wardrobe of Potter-tastic attire out in the Muggle world—and the wearable crafts found in this chapter will definitely get you there!

HOUSE COLORS TIE-DYE SHIRT

This House Colors Tie-Dye Shirt is always really fun when you have a lot of friends over because it's super fast to make and everyone can make a shirt in his or her favorite house colors (scarlet and gold for Gryffindor, yellow and black for Hufflepuff, blue and bronze for Ravenclaw, emerald green and silver for Slytherin) following the same basic steps. Plus, when you're finished, you can all wear them to your next Quidditch game!

WHAT YOU NEED:

Prewashed plain white T-shirt in the size of your choice

10–15 rubber bands (The number you use depends on how big your shirt is and how close together you want your stripes.)

2 tie-dye kits in the colors of your house (Note: each dye kit will contain 1 dye color, gloves, and a squirt bottle.)

1 (16-ounce) bottle of water

Paper towels

2 large trash bags

Scissors

HOW TO MAKE IT:

I. Prepare your shirt by holding it up in front of you and scrunching it into a long tube.

2. Once it's scrunched, wrap rubber bands around the tube wherever you want the white to show through. (I like to use the white as a barrier in between my stripes.)

3. Put on the gloves that came in the dye kit, then take your water and mix your dyes in the kits' squirt bottles according to package instructions.

4. Next squirt out a little of your two dye colors on some paper towels to make sure they are the correct colors.

5. Lay down a trash bag to protect your countertop and place your shirt on top of it. (This part is messy, so you can even do it outside.)

6. Starting with your first color (I wanted a Gryffindor shirt, so I started with red dye), squirt your dye straight onto the shirt, at the top. Be sure to saturate your shirt, but don't use so much dye that it bleeds into other parts of the fabric.

7. Then take your second dye color (I used yellow) and squirt that onto your shirt.

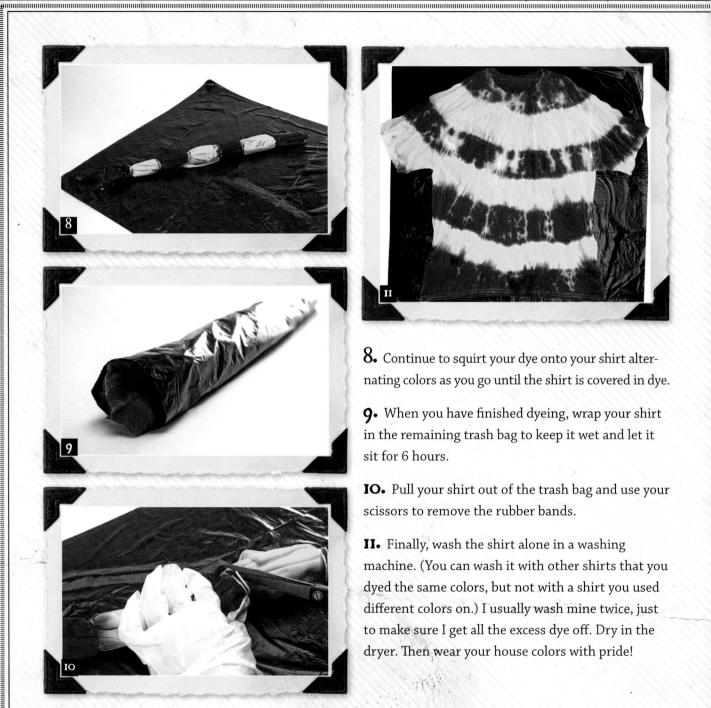

8. Continue to squirt your dye onto your shirt alternating colors as you go until the shirt is covered in dye.

9. When you have finished dyeing, wrap your shirt in the remaining trash bag to keep it wet and let it sit for 6 hours.

IO. Pull your shirt out of the trash bag and use your scissors to remove the rubber bands.

II. Finally, wash the shirt alone in a washing machine. (You can wash it with other shirts that you dyed the same colors, but not with a shirt you used different colors on.) I usually wash mine twice, just to make sure I get all the excess dye off. Dry in the dryer. Then wear your house colors with pride!

TRANSFIGURATION TIPS

Personalize your shirt by choosing your
Hogwarts house colors. If you're a Hufflepuff,
buy yellow and black dye kits. If you're a
Gryffindor, buy red and yellow dye kits.
If you're a Ravenclaw, buy blue and orange
dye kits. If you're a Slytherin, buy green and
black dye kits. (Note: Slytherin's colors are
actually green and silver, so you'll want to buy
a black dye kit, but only use half the
dye that the kit calls for. This should give
you the silvery/gray color that
you're looking for.)

SUGAR QUILL HEADBAND

Sugar quill wasn't just a password to get inside Dumbledore's office; it was also his favorite candy. If I could figure out how to make my own pens taste like candy, like a sugar quill, I would. But for now we will just have to make do with a Sugar Quill Headband. This project is simple enough that you can make one for you and every Harry Potter fan you know.

WHAT YOU NEED:

1 plastic headband

1 (5") feather (It doesn't matter which color you choose, but I used purple.)

Hot glue gun and glue

HOW TO MAKE IT:

1

2

1. To start, put the headband on your head and hold the feather up next to it to figure out the correct placement. The feather should be to the side, but not so far down that it ends up covered in hair. I placed my feather about 3" up from the bottom of the headband. You want your feather facing up, so the feathery part sticks up and the shaft is down toward the bottom of your headband. Then take off the headband while still holding the feather in place.

2. Lift the feather slightly off the headband, and use your glue gun to place a few drops of glue on the headband that run the length of the feather.

3. Press the feather onto the headband, and try not to let the glue show. You might need to add glue to the top and bottom of the feather as well, just to get it to curve along the headband.

4. Now, make enough of these to wear a different color every day of the week!

TRANSFIGURATION TIPS

You don't have to use this technique on headbands. You can also attach the feather to an alligator clip and use it as a barrette, or attach it to a leather bracelet and make a wristband. Also, this craft and a lot of these crafts throughout the book use a glue gun. If you're not comfortable using one of those, then tacky glue and a little bit of drying time will work just as well.

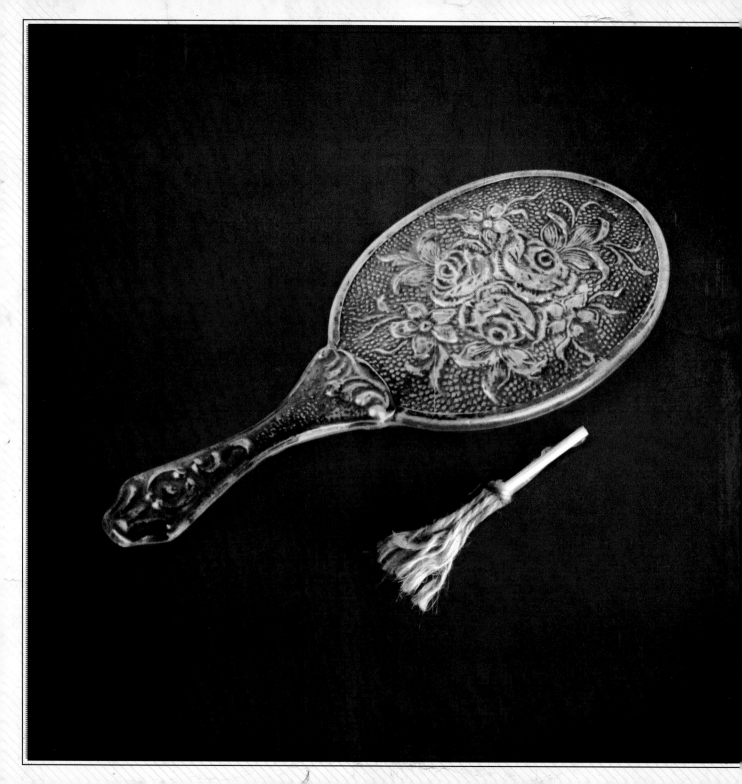

NIMBUS TWO THOUSAND HAIRPIN

Maybe you don't have a flying broomstick, or maybe yours is in the shop. Either way, this Nimbus Two Thousand Hairpin is where it's at. I wear mine to all the fancy events, both wizarding and Muggle.

WHAT YOU NEED:

1 wooden skewer (like you would find in the grilling section of the grocery store)

1 bobby pin

Hot glue gun and glue

2 or 3 (1") pieces of hemp or twine

1 (1¼") piece of hemp or twine

HOW TO MAKE IT:

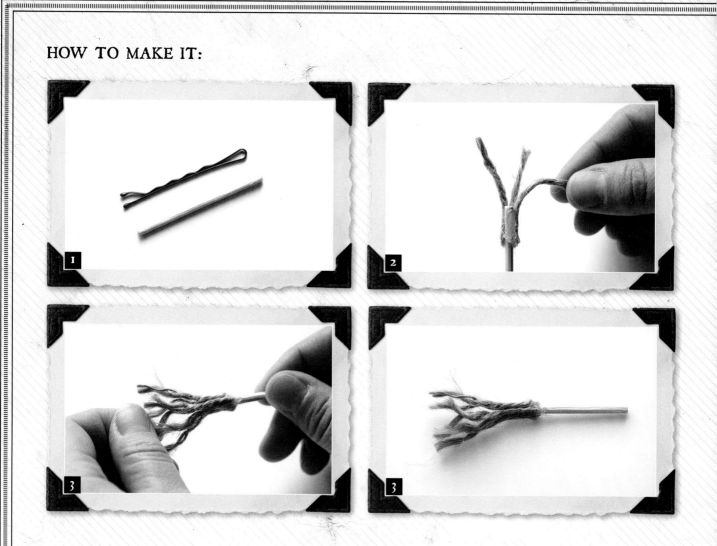

1. Break your skewer to be about the same size as your bobby pin (don't use the pointy end; you want to use the flat end).

2. Use the hot glue gun to glue the ends of your 1" pieces of twine to the end of the skewer. Press the twine to the skewer for a few seconds to make sure it's secure.

3. Take the ends of the twine you haven't glued down and fray them out about ½" so that they look like the end of a broom.

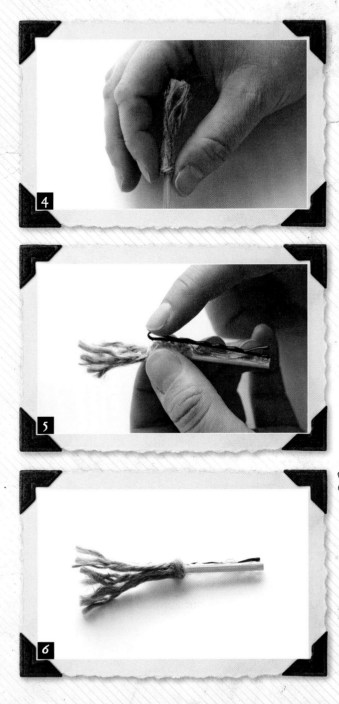

4. Put a small dab of glue at the center of the 1¼" piece of twine and glue it perpendicular to the skewer, where the twine and the skewer meet, so it looks like it's holding together the broom.

5. Glue your broom across the entire surface of the bobby pin and hold it for just a couple of seconds until the glue sets.

6. You now have a Nimbus Two Thousand Hairpin that everyone else will be totally jealous of. Wear it and enjoy!

TRANSFIGURATION TIPS

If you prefer, you can also glue your broom to an alligator clip for a little more stability.

GOLDEN SNITCH NECKLACE

The Golden Snitch is the most important part of any Quidditch match, which makes the Golden Snitch Necklace one of my favorite pieces of jewelry to create. It's important to follow the directions exactly, or you might end up with one of your wings upside down or flipped around backwards!

WHAT YOU NEED:

Jewelry wire cutters

1 (19") small gold chain

Tiny jewelry pliers

1 small gold jewelry clasp (I used a lobster clasp, but you can use whatever you like best or whatever you can find at your local craft store.)

4 (5 mm) gold jump rings

1 (3"-long) gold eyepin (The thickness doesn't matter as long as it fits through your gold bead.)

1 gold ball bead (The hole in this bead needs to be big enough that you can fit your wire through it.)

2 (½"-long) gold wing charms

HOW TO MAKE IT:

I. Use your wire cutters to cut your small gold chain into 2 even pieces of 9½" each.

2. Next use your jewelry pliers to open a jump ring. Do this by grasping the jump ring with the pliers, making sure the split in the ring faces up, and holding the other side of the ring with your fingers. Now slowly and gently twist the pliers toward you and twist your other hand away from you.

3. Thread the open jump ring through the last link of one of the jewelry chains.

4. Now thread the small loop on the end of the jewelry clasp through this same jump ring. Use your jewelry pliers to squeeze the jump ring closed by holding one side of the ring with the pliers and the other with your fingers. Twist the sides toward each other to bring them together and close the ring.

5. Use your jewelry pliers to open your second jump ring. Thread the last link of the other jewelry chain (the one without the clasp) through the jump ring and then use your pliers to close the ring. Your clasp will attach to this ring to connect the finished necklace ends.

6. Run the gold eyepin through the gold bead.

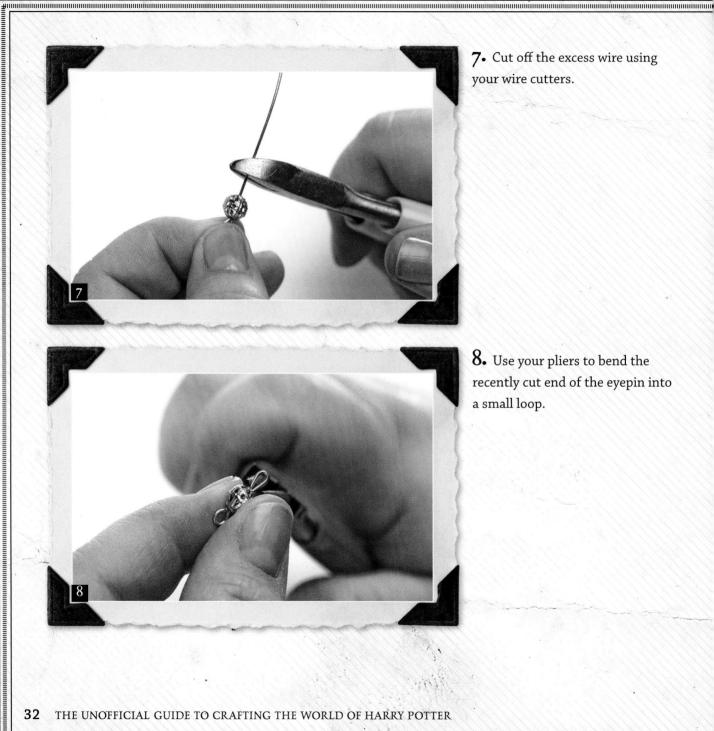

7. Cut off the excess wire using your wire cutters.

8. Use your pliers to bend the recently cut end of the eyepin into a small loop.

9. Arrange your necklace pieces as shown in the photo. This is how the necklace will fit together.

10. Open a third jump ring and thread it through the tip of one of your gold wing charms. Then thread the last link of one of the chains through the jump ring. Close the jump ring. Repeat this using your fourth jump ring, the other gold wing charm, and the other half of the necklace.

II. Open the jump ring that came attached to the gold wing charm. Thread the ring through one of the loops on the gold bead. Close the ring. Repeat this using the other gold wing charm and the other loop on the gold bead.

12. Now you have the cutest little snitch necklace ever! Wear it and enjoy.

TRANSFIGURATION TIPS

You can decide how long you
want your necklace to be.
Just cut your chain to
whatever size
you want!

LIGHTNING SCAR EARRINGS

Harry's scar is a big deal, and so are these Lightning Scar Earrings! You can use them to top off your Potter-themed outfit, or you can just wear them on their own. And if you want to branch out beyond the scar, you can make all sorts of different Potter-tastic symbols like glasses, scarves, or even a Deathly Hallows symbol!

WHAT YOU NEED:

1 Shrinky Dinks sheet

Colored pencil (I used black, but you can use any color you like.)

Scissors

Parchment paper

Cookie sheet

Spatula

Hot glue gun and glue

2 flat earring posts and earring backs (It doesn't matter what size or color, and when you buy the posts, they will come with backs.)

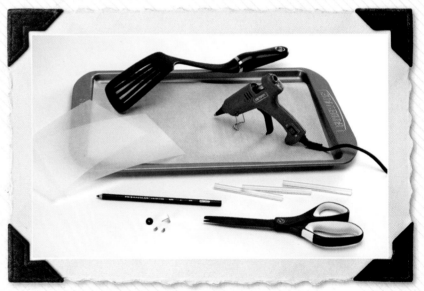

1. Preheat the oven to 325°F, then use a colored pencil to draw 2 same-sized lightning bolts on the rough side of your Shrinky Dinks paper. Make sure to draw these about three times larger than you want your earrings to be as these will shrink in the oven.

2. On the rough side of the Shrinky Dinks paper, color in the lightning bolts with your colored pencil, then use your scissors to cut them out. Take your time cutting them out, because you want them to look awesome.

3. Place the parchment paper on the cookie sheet, then lay your lightning bolts on the parchment paper rough side up, making sure they don't touch. (They will melt together if they do.) Bake them for 1–3 minutes in the oven. You have to watch them while they bake. They will curl up while they are shrinking and then flatten out.

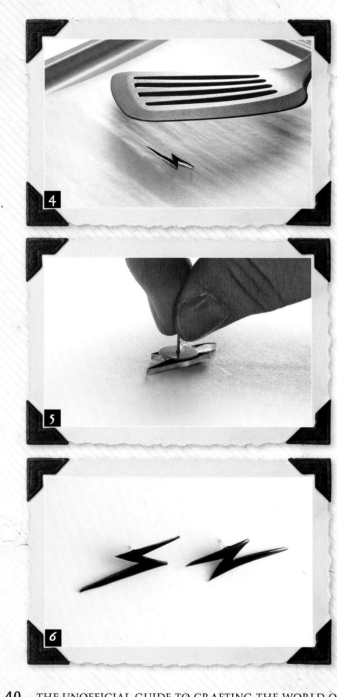

4. When they've flattened out, pull them out of the oven and use your spatula to push down and make sure they are super flat. Let them sit for 5 minutes or until cool to the touch.

5. Use your glue gun to glue the earring posts to the back of your lightning bolts. (Note: the back is the rough/duller side that you colored with your pencils.) Hold the earring posts to the lightning bolts for a few seconds until the glue sets up.

6. Once your glue is hard, your Lightning Scar Earrings are ready to wear!

TRANSFIGURATION TIPS

If earrings aren't your thing, feel
free to make lightning scar key
chains instead! All you need to do
is make a small hole in the charm
and then slip it on a key ring
and you'll have Harry Potter
with you whenever you
use your keys.

REMEMBRALL RING

Always feel like you are forgetting something? It's most likely because you are. Wear your forgetfulness proudly with this Remembrall Ring! Neville Longbottom received a Remembrall, a ball that fills with red smoke when the user has forgotten something, from his gran in *Harry Potter and the Sorcerer's Stone*. This ring may not fill with smoke, but it's still the perfect way to remember everything that is important without being too obvious! I love that it looks so pretty it could be a piece of jewelry with no purpose at all, but you should only wear it when you have something you can't forget!

WHAT YOU NEED:

1 (20 mm) screw glass globe ring (You can buy these in the jewelry section of your craft store or online.)

1 thin gold-plated jewelry chain

Hot glue gun and and glue

Wire cutters

Red glitter

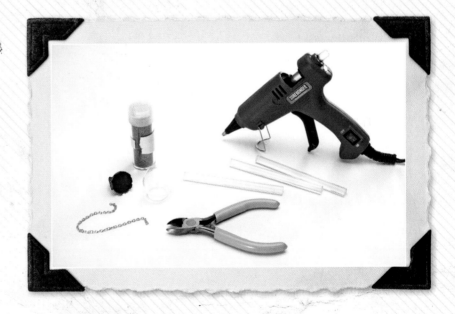

HOW TO MAKE IT:

I. Use your hot glue gun to carefully glue the gold chain to one side of the globe's base. Be sure to put the glue on the globe, not on the cap. Press the chain into the glue for a few seconds until it begins to set up. Then add glue in a line stretching across the top of the globe, making sure the line is placed slightly off center. Stretch the chain across the top of the globe onto the line of glue and press the chain into the glue for a few seconds until it begins to set up. Then, glue the other end of the chain to the base on the other side of the globe. Again, be sure to glue on the globe, not on the cap. Press the chain into the glue for a few seconds until it begins to set up.

2. Once the glue has dried, use your wire cutters to cut away any extra length of chain.

3. Next fill the glass globe with the red glitter.

4. Use your glue gun to add glue to the inside of the ring's base.

5. Screw the cap back on to attach it to the ring's base, and wait for the glue to dry, about 30 seconds.

6. Wear your Remembrall Ring with pride—and try to remember what it was you forgot!

TRANSFIGURATION TIPS

This ring is really big.
When you wear it, be
careful not to get it caught
on everything!

CHAPTER 2

THE RESTRICTED SECTION OF THE LIBRARY: CRAFTS FOR SCHOOL

—◆—

Everyone knows that the library has all the best books, but did you know that the Restricted Section of the library is where they hide all the super-cool Potter-tastic wizarding school supplies that everyone wants? (Okay, so maybe that isn't entirely true, but for the purposes of this book, that's where you can find them!)

I take all my notes in a Spellbook Journal, and I keep my paper clips in a Pensieve Paper Clip Dish. It's a fun way to make my workspace all my own! One of my favorite things about all these supplies is that they aren't overly Potter-rific, so you can still use them every single day and only the true fans will know you are nerding out.

SPELLBOOK JOURNAL

Every good wizard knows that you need a place to keep all the spells you are learning while you're at school, and this Spellbook Journal is perfect for that! It takes a little while to make, because you have to wait on the layers of paint to dry, but when you see how much like a real spellbook this is, it is totally worth it!

WHAT YOU NEED:

1 (8½" × 11") sheet of computer paper with the word "SPELLBOOK" printed on it (I used the Georgia font and made my letters a variety of different font sizes, ranging from 54 to 62 pts, so that the word looks more hand stamped.)

Tape

Composition book

Pencil

Foam paintbrush, any size

1 color of acrylic paint (Think spooky, spell-tastic colors, like green or purple.)

Gold paint pen

Brown distress ink pad

Mod Podge

HOW TO MAKE IT:

1. Tape the printed page with the word "SPELLBOOK" on it to the front cover of your composition book toward the top and trace over the word hard with a pencil. (You are trying to make an indentation in your composition book so it looks like the words are stamped into it.)

2. Peel the taped page off your book. Open the composition book, lay it flat on a hard surface, and paint the outside cover with your foam paintbrush and acrylic paint. Once the book is completely painted, let it dry thoroughly, about 1–2 hours. Depending on your paint, you might have to paint 2 or 3 coats, but you should make sure your book is dry in between the coats.

3. Use the gold paint pen to trace the indented letters, then color them in and let them dry for 10–15 minutes.

4. When the paint has dried, use your gold paint pen to add a couple of gold stripes to the spine of your book.

5. Then, use the gold paint pen to add a swirl about the same size as your title to the front cover underneath the writing.

6. Go over the edges of your book with the brown distress ink to give it an aged feel. You do this by putting the stamp pad straight onto the edges of the book and gliding it up and down. Remember, these spellbooks have been around forever!

7. Use the paintbrush to cover the book with Mod Podge, painting over everything to seal in your design. Let that dry overnight.

8. Once the Mod Podge has dried, enjoy! You have the best Spellbook Journal ever!

HALLECAKE SAYS

I can always tell that these composition books are mine, and for some reason they make science class way easier!

PENCIL WAND

This Pencil Wand is so much more than just a wand. It's the perfect thing to use to write in your Spellbook Journal (see project in this chapter). Plus, it is so unique that nobody will ever steal your pencil and forget to give it back. These are fun to give to your friends so you can have secret wizard battles in class that nobody knows about.

WHAT YOU NEED:

1 unsharpened pencil

Hot glue gun and glue

*2 or 3 colors of acrylic paint
(I used brown, red, and gold.)*

1 paper plate

2 or 3 (1") foam paintbrushes

2 disposable plastic cups

Mod Podge

HOW TO MAKE IT:

I. Starting at the eraser end of your pencil, swirl hot glue around the pencil about ¼ of the way down. To do this, it's easier to hold the hot glue gun while you twist the pencil around. Hold this in the air until the glue dries, about 1 minute.

2. Squeeze a silver-dollar-sized dab of your first color of acrylic paint onto a paper plate. Add a second silver-dollar-sized dab of your second color right next to the first color. Continue until you've added one dab of each paint color onto your plate. Then use your finger to gently swirl the colors together. You want to end up with a pinwheel of your different colors, not create a brown or black paint.

3. Take your paintbrush, dip it in your swirled paint, and paint your entire pencil. Paint right over the hot glue so that it looks like the handle of your wand is hand carved out of wood.

4. To ensure that all sides of your pencil will dry evenly, take your plastic cups and place them right side up so that the rims are touching. Place your pencil on top of the cups and leave it there to dry thoroughly, about 4–5 hours.

5. If your wand still isn't fully covered in paint and a little glue is showing through, add an additional coat of paint to fully cover the pencil and hot glue. Once the second coat of paint has been added, place your pencil on top of the cups and set aside to dry to the touch, about 1 hour.

6. When your Pencil Wand is fairly dry to the touch, use a clean paintbrush to add a coat of Mod Podge over any painted parts to seal in the design and protect it. Place your pencil on top of the cups and set it aside to dry overnight.

7. Finally, sharpen your pencil and try not to accidentally cast any spells while you're journaling away!

HALLECAKE SAYS

———————

You can choose to cover your eraser to make your pencil look more like a wand, or leave it so you can have a pencil that erases. Expelliarmus!

MONSTER BOOK OF MONSTERS
TABLET COVER

There's pretty much nothing cooler than opening up your *Monster Book of Monsters* Tablet Cover. It's crazy adorable, and you will always be able to tell your tablet from everyone else's! If you don't have a cover for your tablet, you can cover the backside of the tablet in painter's tape and just make a one-sided cover without damaging your electronics. With this super-fun project, you get a super-cool book without the threat of losing any of your fingers.

WHAT YOU NEED:

Cover for your tablet (I used an old one that was all beat up and looked terrible. It doesn't matter because you are going to cover it in fur anyway.)

1 (24" × 24") piece of faux fur (You can find this at a craft store.)

Scissors

Heavy-duty double-sided tape, any width (You want the really strong stuff that is designed to stick to fabric. You can find it at any craft store.)

Hot glue gun and glue

Pointy rubber teeth (I actually ordered some online, but if it's around Halloween, you can find these all over the place.)

4 large googly eyes (I used yellow ones because I thought that looked more monster-tastic.)

HOW TO MAKE IT:

I. Place your open tablet cover onto the back of the faux fur and cut around it so that your fur is approximately the same size as the cover. Leave a little extra fur on all the edges. It's supposed to be big and monster-like, so it's okay if it hangs off the edge a bit.

2. Outline the edges of the backside of your open tablet cover with the double-sided tape, then add a few additional pieces to the middle and to the spine of the cover.

3. Remove the backing on the double-sided tape.

4. Then close up the tablet cover and drape the faux fur, flat side down, over the front and back of the cover, pressing on the fur to secure.

5. If your tablet cover has a closure tab, use your scissors to remove it.

6. Use your scissors to cut off the backside of the mouth guard on your monster teeth so the teeth will lay flat against the edge of the tablet cover.

7. Use your glue gun to secure the top part of your teeth to the middle of the front side edge of the cover and the bottom part to the middle of the back side edge so that they look like they are chomping down together when you close it. Hold the teeth down for a few seconds so the glue dries.

8. Use your glue gun to glue 4 googly eyes to the top part of the cover just above the teeth, so they look like the monster's eyes, and hold them in place for a few seconds until completely dry.

9. Have fun scaring yourself with your super-awesome *Monster Book of Monsters* Tablet Cover!

HALLECAKE SAYS

This is definitely my favorite project in this chapter. It's perfect because I changed all my friends' names in my tablet to HP characters anyway, so I might as well show those off!

PENSIEVE PAPER CLIP DISH

Okay, so maybe this Pensieve doesn't hold all your most precious memories or anything, but it does hold paper clips, and that's equally as important when we are talking about a super-cool homework station. I love how this dish is just a subtle nod to Potter, so you can keep your fandom under wraps and still display it proudly. I also like that the marbling effect means nobody will ever make one that looks exactly like yours—which is how memories should be—plus when you're struggling with your homework, maybe you can use your Pensieve to jog your own memory!

WHAT YOU NEED:

Small, flat-ish dish, about 2"–3" in diameter

Fine-grit sandpaper (optional)

1 paper towel (optional)

Silver, purple, and black nail polish

Silver glitter nail polish

2 or 3 toothpicks

HOW TO MAKE IT:

1. If your dish is really slick, give it a few brushes with sandpaper and then wipe off any excess dust with a dry paper towel.

2. Use the brush in the nail polish to drip 5 or 6 drops each of the silver and purple nail polishes into the basin of your dish. Then drip 5 or 6 drops of the sliver glitter nail polish and 2 or 3 drops of the black polish into the basin of the dish.

3. Use a toothpick to swirl the nail polish around in the dish until the surface of the dish is covered. Be careful when you're doing this, because you want the colors to swirl together, not mix all up into a boring gray. If you feel that your colors are becoming muddied, swap out the toothpick you're using for a fresh one until you're happy with the swirl.

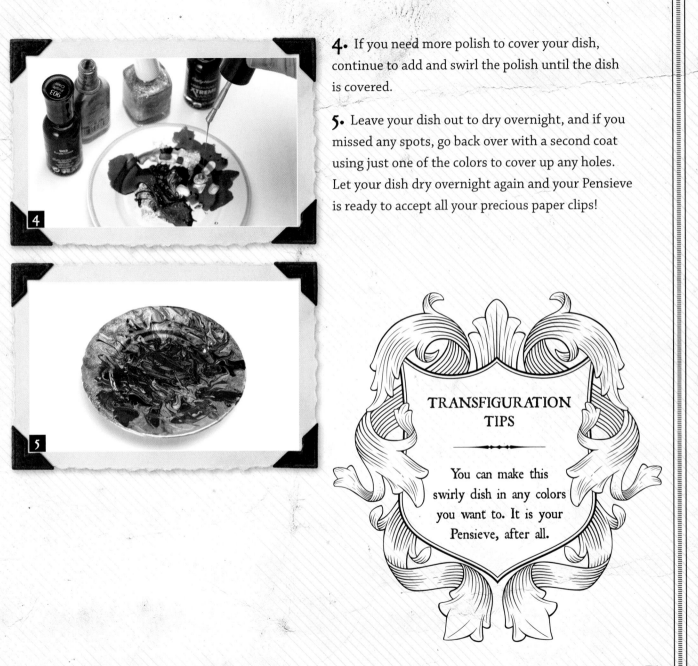

4. If you need more polish to cover your dish, continue to add and swirl the polish until the dish is covered.

5. Leave your dish out to dry overnight, and if you missed any spots, go back over with a second coat using just one of the colors to cover up any holes. Let your dish dry overnight again and your Pensieve is ready to accept all your precious paper clips!

TRANSFIGURATION TIPS

You can make this swirly dish in any colors you want to. It is your Pensieve, after all.

MANDRAKE ROOT PENCIL HOLDER

The root to any good spell starts with a pencil, which is kind of crazy when you think about it, because pencils are made from trees—which have roots. This little Mandrake Root Pencil Holder—a nod to the plant with the fatal screams introduced in *Harry Potter and the Chamber of Secrets*—is way too cool to just sit in your room! Make sure you put it out for everyone to see.

WHAT YOU NEED:

1 (16-ounce) POM Wonderful 100% Pomegranate Juice bottle (washed and dried)

Serrated knife

1 medium-sized cardboard box or trash bag

Beige/cream spray paint

Scissors

1 or 2 curly willow branches

Hot glue gun and glue

10–18 mini green artificial leaves

2 small black buttons or googly eyes

HOW TO MAKE IT:

1. Carefully use a serrated knife to cut off the top of the bottle (including the cap). This is sharp, so make sure to have an adult help you out with this part! All you will have left are the 2 rounded bulbs of the bottle; it kind of looks like a snowman.

2. Next, set up a place to spray-paint your bottle by placing your cardboard box or trash bag on the floor or outside on the ground. (Ask an adult for help if you're not sure where this should be done.) Place your plastic bottle in the box or on the trash bag and spray it with the beige spray paint until it's completely covered. Then set the bottle aside to dry, about 1 hour. If you painted your bottle outside and would like it to dry inside, let it sit for 15 minutes until dry to the touch, then bring it in to dry completely in an out-of-the-way location.

3. While that's drying, use your scissors to cut 5 or 6 (5"–6") pieces of the curly willow branch.

4. Use your hot glue gun to attach 2 or 3 green leaves to one end of each of the branch pieces. Hold them in place a few seconds to dry. Then, if necessary, wrap the leaf stems around the branch pieces to secure.

5. Once the POM bottle has dried, use your glue gun to attach the 5 or 6 curly willow branches with the leaves vertically onto the backside of the bottle so that they peek over the top of the bottle like branches. Hold them in place a few seconds to dry.

6. Use your scissors to cut 4 smaller (2") pieces of curly willow branches.

7. Use your hot glue gun to attach the small branches onto the front bottom of the POM bottle so that they stick out like feet. You want to be careful here, because you still want your bottle to stand upright.

8. Use your glue gun to attach the buttons or googly eyes to the front part of your bottle near the top and allow to dry for a few seconds.

9. Once the eyes are dry, your Mandrake Root Pencil Holder is ready to hold all your pencils!

TRANSFIGURATION TIPS

Instead of making this into a pencil holder, you could add a flower and some dirt for a super-cool planter!

SORCERER'S STONE PAPERWEIGHT

Remember when Harry had to desire having the Sorcerer's Stone in his pocket in order for it to appear? Well, you don't have to do that to make this project and use it to keep your homework organized on your desk. Get your materials for this craft, sit down in front of your favorite Harry Potter movie (mine is *Harry Potter and the Goblet of Fire*), and get ready to start gluing!

WHAT YOU NEED:

1 (5-pound) bag of red aquarium rocks

Hot glue gun and glue

HOW TO MAKE IT:

1. Take a couple of small aquarium rocks and use your hot glue gun to glue them together.

2. Continue to glue the rocks together a couple at a time until you have a stone that is almost the same size as the palm of your hand. Then set the stone aside to cool for a few minutes.

3. Once the glue is dry, pull all the strings out from the excess glue.

4. Finally, put your totally awesome Sorcerer's Stone Paperweight on top of the papers on your desk to stay organized with style!

HALLECAKE SAYS

While my mom was making this, I just painted a rock bright red and dipped it in glitter. It looked pretty cool, too. You could try that if you wanted to make a whole bunch of these for gifts or whatever.

CHAPTER 3

THE PREFECTS' BATHROOM: CRAFTS FOR STYLE

The prefects' bathroom is the place to find all the primo style items for looking amazing. How else could the prefects always look so perfect?

After a long day of spell casting and fending themselves off against the Dark Lord, wizards need to take care of themselves. So to look your best, in true wizarding style, these are for you. There are so many fun products in here to make and try that you will be Potter-rific in no time. The Dragon Scale Face Paints are so rich and sparkly when you wear them, and I love giving the Potion Lotion and the Pygmy Puff Bath Fizzies as gifts to all my Potter-crazed friends!

BUTTERBEER LIP BALM

This Butterbeer Lip Balm will have you tasting that butterbeer flavor all day long. I don't know a better way to feel Potter-tastic than that. So whenever you find yourself wishing for the sweet treats in Hogsmeade, just pull out your Butterbeer Lip Balm and picture yourself at the Three Broomsticks with Harry, Ron, and Hermione.

WHAT YOU NEED:

1 tablespoon beeswax (You can use either the grated stuff or pellets. I usually order mine online.)

1 teaspoon honey

5–7 butterscotch chips (found in the baking aisle at your local supermarket)

1 tablespoon coconut oil (found in the organic section of your local supermarket)

1 small bowl

1 spoon

3–5 lip balm containers (I like the little clear pots so you can see your lip balm, but you can also use the clear tubes.)

HOW TO MAKE IT:

THE UNOFFICIAL GUIDE TO CRAFTING THE WORLD OF HARRY POTTER

1. Add the beeswax, honey, butterscotch chips, and coconut oil to a small bowl.

2. Melt the ingredients in the microwave in 15-second increments. Pull out in between and stir the mixture with a spoon. When everything is melted together, with no lumps, you're ready to move on to the next step.

3. When your ingredients have all melted together, slowly pour your mixture into the lip balm containers and set aside to cool for 15–20 minutes or until the mixture has hardened.

4. Once the mixture has hardened, put the lid on your Butterbeer Lip Balm and start using immediately! If you'd like, you can give the others out to all your friends or store in a cool cabinet for up to 6 months!

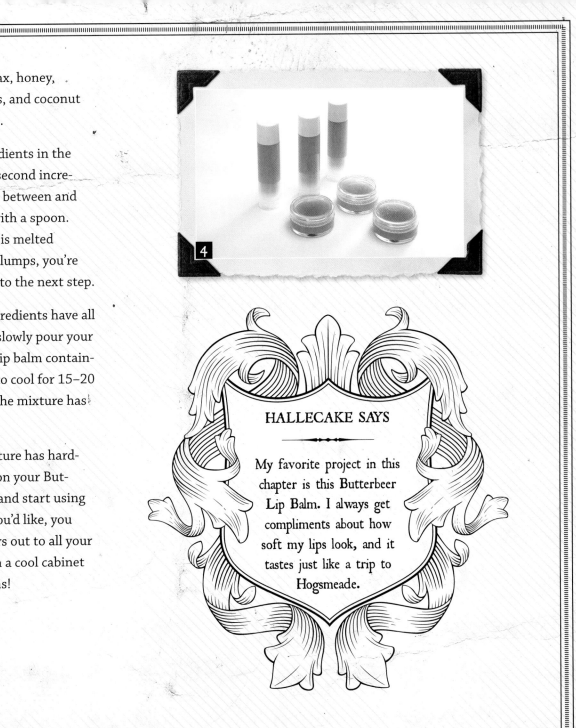

HALLECAKE SAYS

My favorite project in this chapter is this Butterbeer Lip Balm. I always get compliments about how soft my lips look, and it tastes just like a trip to Hogsmeade.

PYGMY PUFF BATH FIZZIES

Pygmy Puffs are arguably the craziest thing about all the Harry Potter books. And these bath fizzies are just as crazy. They are fun to make and even more fun to watch fizz in the tub! This will make 5 or 6 bath bombs, and you might as well make the whole batch, because Pygmy Puff Bath Fizzies are awesome!

WHAT YOU NEED:

1 large bowl

½ cup citric acid

1 cup baking soda

½ teaspoon olive oil

2 or 3 tablespoons witch hazel (in a spray bottle)

2 or 3 drops purple liquid food dye

10 or 12 black sugar pearls

1 (12-cup) silicone mini muffin pan

HOW TO MAKE IT:

1. In a large bowl, combine citric acid and baking soda.

2. Add the olive oil and stir to combine.

3. Spray your bath fizzy mixture with witch hazel. You just need a few quick sprays to make sure everything holds together well.

4. Add the food dye and stir until everything is evenly coated.

5. Press the mixture firmly into 5–6 of the muffin tin cups.

6. Press 2 black sugar pearls into the top of each of the fizzies. (These are the Pygmy Puff eyes.)

7. Let the mixture dry overnight, then pop the Pygmy Puff Bath Fizzies out of their molds.

8. Run a bath and use these fun fizzies immediately or store them in an airtight container for up to 1 year.

TRANSFIGURATION TIPS

———

Your Pygmy Puffs can be any color! Try adding in different dyes. You could use black dye to make Dark Arts Bath Fizzies, or pink and yellow to make more fun-colored Pygmy Puffs!

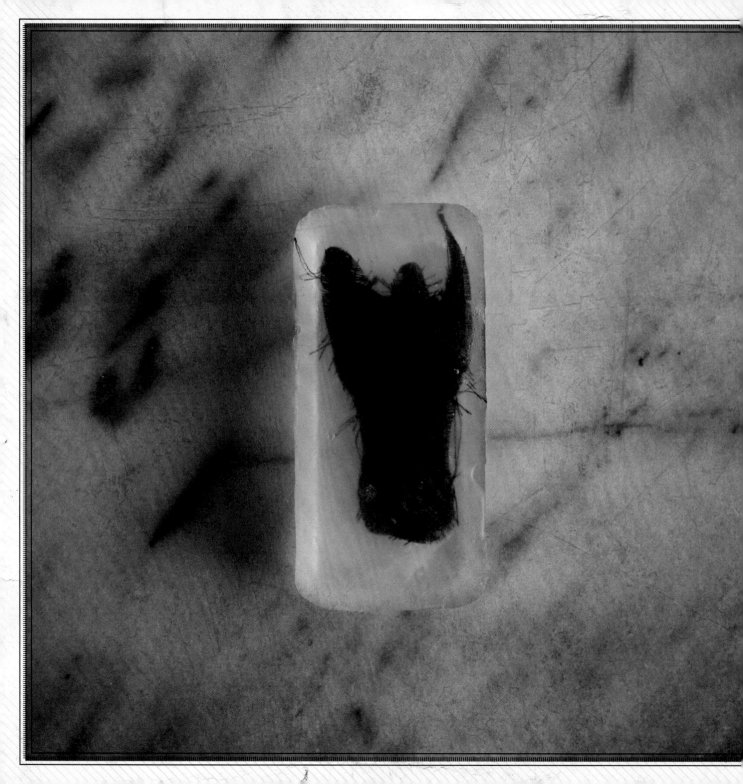

DEMENTOR SOAP

(by Brittanie Pyper from *Simplistically Living* blog at *http://simplisticallyliving.com*)

After a long day of spells and wandering through the woods, you will need a way to wash off all that dirt! What better way than with Dementor Soap! This stuff is as creepy cool as it sounds.

WHAT YOU NEED:

6 (3" × 2") pieces of black fabric (Cotton will work best.)

Scissors

Serrated knife

2 pounds clear melt and pour soap base (This can be bought online.)

2 microwave-safe measuring cups (or bowls)

Tea towel (optional)

Spoon

6-cavity rectangle (3.1" × 2.2" × 1") silicone soap mold (You can get these online, and most craft stores have them, too.)

2 or 3 tablespoons isopropyl alcohol (in a spray bottle)

HOW TO MAKE IT:

1. Take your pieces of black fabric and use your scissors to make them look ripped, torn, and kind of ghost-like. (Remember, the idea here is to make it look like a dementor. So you don't need eyes or a mouth, just an outline of the shape.) Set them aside.

2. Next, use your knife to cut the soap base into 1" × 1" cubes. Note: most soap bases have prescored lines that you can and should cut along. This can be dangerous, so make sure to have an adult help you out with this part! Keep about 5 pieces of soap aside, and place the rest into your microwave-safe cup or bowl.

3. Microwave for 30 seconds, then remove and stir with a spoon. Continue doing this until all of the soap is melted.

4. If the bowl is hot, hold it with a tea towel and pour the soap equally into each cavity of your mold, filling them about ⅔ of the way full. The soap can get pretty hot, so if you're uncomfortable with pouring it yourself, please ask a grownup for help.

5. Spray with the isopropyl alcohol to remove any air bubbles from the surface. Leave uncovered and allow this to harden for about 1 hour.

6. Once your soap is hard, spray the top of the soap with isopropyl alcohol again and also spray the black fabric with 2 or 3 sprays of alcohol.

7. As you did in Step 3, melt your remaining 5 pieces of soap in the microwave in 30-second increments until melted, then pour half of the soap mixture into another cup or bowl and set aside. Using one bowlful of the mixture, pour a tiny amount of melted soap on top of the hardened soap in each cavity so you can place the fabric in it without it moving around.

8. Now gently place the fabric dementors on the top middle of the melted soap in each cavity. Work quickly because this layer will harden fast.

9. Once you have the fabric in the middle of your molds, pour the remaining melted soap on top of the fabric until each cavity is completely filled.

10. Spray the top of the soap with isopropyl alcohol and allow to harden overnight.

11. When the soap has hardened, remove it from the mold by gently pushing from the back of the mold until the soap pops out.

12. Use your soap immediately or wrap in plastic wrap and store for up to a year in a cool, dry place.

TRANSFIGURATION TIPS

Instead of adding fabric to your soap, try adding a plastic frog to make Honeydukes soap or a snake to make Parseltongue soap. It makes for a fun treat when you use up all the soap!

POTION LOTION

You won't find the recipe for this Potion Lotion in *Advanced Potion-Making* (as Snape would say), even though the Half-Blood Prince could've definitely used some, but you will find that it makes your skin feel silky smooth and smell good. And if you want to know how, well, it's magic. The best part of this is that you can reuse the fancy potion bottles again and again when you run out of lotion. This recipe will make about a cup of lotion, so you may need more or less depending on your container.

WHAT YOU NEED:

Large bowl

1 cup coconut oil

1 teaspoon vitamin E oil (You can either buy a bottle or just use the capsules from the pharmacy. They're easy to open up and pour the oil out of.)

2 or 3 drops liquid food dye (I like to use purple or green, but any color is fine; you just want it to look like a potion.)

Hand mixer

Lotion bottles or containers (You want your bottles to look like something you would keep a potion in. I found mine at the dollar store.)

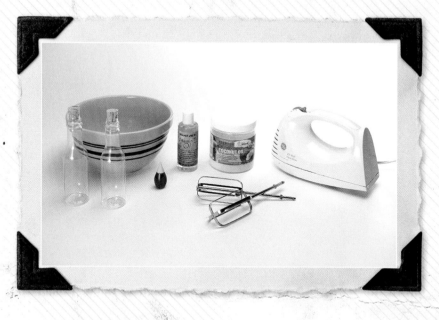

HOW TO MAKE IT:

I. In a large bowl, combine the coconut oil, vitamin E, and your liquid food dye.

2. Use your hand mixer and mix on medium speed for 2–3 minutes until you reach a creamy, lotion-like consistency.

3. Pour the mixture into your lotion bottles and store in a cool, dark place. This lotion should keep for up to 3 months.

HALLECAKE SAYS

This is one of my fave things
to give to my teachers. I am
pretty sure that all teachers
love Harry Potter.
Especially Snape!

DRAGON SCALE FACE PAINTS

You know what's cool? Dragon scales. I love how they are all shimmery and sparkly in the light and look like they are a billion different colors, but are also still totally dark and mysterious. I am obsessed with making my own face paint, and this project is so cool because you can make 2 different colors that when applied look just like a dragon's scale—which is perfect if you have to go up against a Chinese Fireball or a Hungarian Horntail in the Triwizard Tournament.

WHAT YOU NEED:

Black Face Paint

Scissors

3–5 charcoal capsules (You can find these at a health store or online.)

1 small bowl

½ teaspoon silver diamond dust mica

1 spoon

1 clear lip balm container

Green Face Paint

2–3 teaspoons powdered spirulina (You can find this at a health store or online.)

1 small bowl

½ teaspoon gold diamond dust mica

1 spoon

1 clear lip balm container

HOW TO MAKE IT:

I. **For Black Face Paint:** Use the scissors to open up your charcoal capsules and pour into the bowl.

2. Add ½ teaspoon silver mica to the bowl with the charcoal. Use a spoon to stir to combine.

3. Pour the black powder into a clear lip balm container.

4. **For Green Face Paint:** Pour your powdered spirulina into a bowl. Then add ½ teaspoon gold mica to the bowl. Use a spoon to stir to combine.

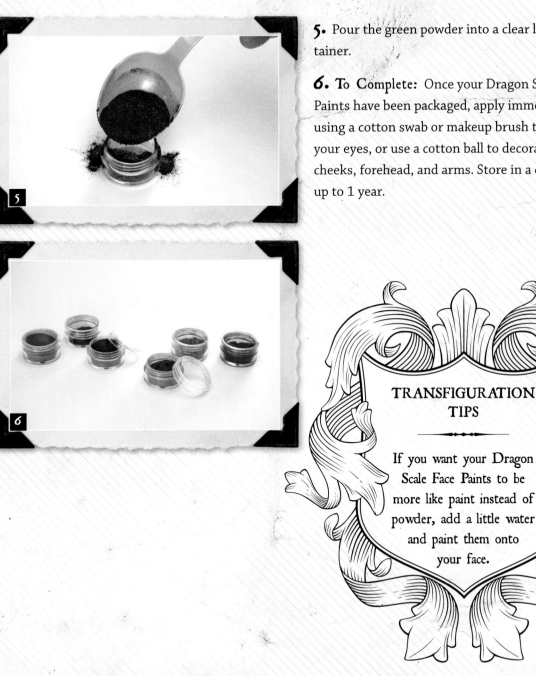

5. Pour the green powder into a clear lip balm container.

6. To Complete: Once your Dragon Scale Face Paints have been packaged, apply immediately by using a cotton swab or makeup brush to put around your eyes, or use a cotton ball to decorate your cheeks, forehead, and arms. Store in a dark place for up to 1 year.

TRANSFIGURATION TIPS

If you want your Dragon Scale Face Paints to be more like paint instead of powder, add a little water and paint them onto your face.

HOUSE COLORS SUGAR SCRUB

All Potter fans know which house they belong in—I'm a Hufflepuff, in case you were wondering—and this House Colors Sugar Scrub is a way to show your house pride and make personalized gifts for your friends and family. This project tells you how to make one jar of sugar scrub, but feel free to double, triple, or quadruple the recipe as needed.

WHAT YOU NEED:

2 cups granulated sugar

1 cup oil (Any oil will work, but grape-seed oil is my favorite because it's clear and doesn't change the color of your scrub.)

2 small bowls

2 spoons

3–5 drops each of 2 colors gel food dye (see house color mixtures in the accompanying sidebar)

1 (32-ounce) clear jar with a lid

HOW TO MAKE IT:

1. Add the sugar and oil to a small bowl and stir to combine.

2. Divide your scrub in half and move half the mixture into another bowl, so you can dye the mix 2 different colors.

3. Add 3–5 drops of your first color dye to one bowl and mix until you get the desired color. Then add 3–5 drops of your second color to your second bowl and mix until you get the desired color.

4. Layer your scrubs one after the other in the jar so it looks like a striped tie or scarf.

5. Close the lid tight and your Hogwarts House Colors Sugar Scrub is complete to give as a gift to your favorite Potter-obsessed friend. (Or keep it for yourself, because it's that awesome.) This will stay fresh up to 1 year in an airtight container.

TRANSFIGURATION TIPS

To get each of the house colors you will need:

- GRYFFINDOR (red and gold):
Add 3-5 drops of red to the first batch.
For the gold, add mostly yellow
and one drop of orange.

- HUFFLEPUFF (yellow and black):
Add 3-5 drops of yellow to the first
batch and 3-5 drops of black to the
second. (Black food dye doesn't usually
come in a kit, but it can be found alone
in the cake-decorating section of your
favorite craft store.)

- RAVENCLAW (blue and bronze): Add 3-5 drops of blue to the first batch and just 1 or 2 drops of yellow to the second. Your sugar might even be off-white enough that you don't have to add any dye to the second batch.

- SLYTHERIN (green and silver): Add 3-5 drops of green to the first batch and just 1 drop of black to the second to give your sugar a silver tint.

CHAPTER 4

THE GREAT HALL: CRAFTS TO USE AROUND THE HOUSE

The Great Hall is where everyone gathers whenever anything important happens, and that's what these crafts are dedicated to: giving you all the right Potter tools to bring everyone together to enjoy good company and good times.

The thing about these projects is that you can use them again and again, to keep Harry Potter in your house year-round. We always try to add a little HP flair to our kitchen and bathroom, because those are the rooms we are in every day, but you'll also love surprising your friends and family with unexpected Harry Potter–themed Potions Ornaments or a silly Chocolate Frog Coaster based on a totally Potter-rific candy!

MARAUDER'S MAP MUG

If you're like me, you need more than just a plain ol' mug to brighten up your day. This Marauder's Map Mug is just the thing to make you laugh—I drink out of mine every morning—and by the time you're finished drinking, your mischief will be managed!

WHAT YOU NEED:

Ivory-colored mug

Brown oil-based paint pen (These are different than regular permanent markers, which will come off even after you cook your mug.)

HOW TO MAKE IT:

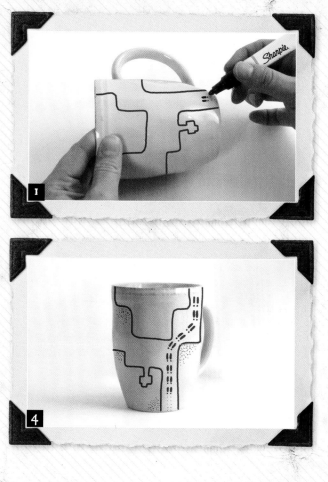

1. On the outside of your coffee mug, draw in the map using your paint pen. This is easy if you think of it as a maze. Draw lines all around your map first, and then add in the footsteps later. You can also add the names of your favorite Potter characters or even your best friend!

2. Once you've finished drawing on your mug, set it aside to dry for 2–3 hours until dry to the touch.

3. Once your mug is dry to the touch, place your mug in the oven, turn your oven on to 325°F, and bake for 30 minutes. Don't preheat your oven; you want to put the mug in while the oven is still cool. After 30 minutes, turn off the oven and let the mug sit in the oven until it's cool enough to touch. (This way your mug won't crack.)

4. Remove your mug from the oven and hand wash in the sink before using. Don't wash your mug in the dishwasher because your writing will come off. You now have a super-cool mug for life!

HALLECAKE SAYS

If you're taking a trip to the Hog's Head, this is the perfect mug to bring.

CHOCOLATE FROG COASTERS

I am pretty sure that Chocolate Frog candies are the most delicious candy anyone has ever tasted. These coasters are a cute way to remember chocolate-covered Ron on his first trip to Hogwarts when Harry bought them tons of candy off the Honeydukes Express trolley on the Hogwarts Express. You can make just a single coaster for you, but this project makes a set of four.

WHAT YOU NEED:

Cardboard box or trash bag

4 (1") plastic toy frogs (You can find these at a dollar store or in the boys' toys section.)

Brown matte spray paint

Scissors or craft knife

1 (16" × 20") cork foam board (You can find this at any local craft store.)

Pencil

2 (12" × 12") sheets of gold shimmer scrapbook paper

1 (1") foam paintbrush

Mod Podge

Hot glue gun and glue

HOW TO MAKE IT:

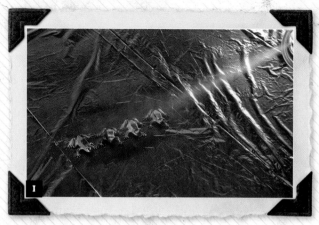

I. Set up a place to spray-paint your frogs by placing your cardboard box or trash bag on the floor or outside on the ground. (Ask an adult for help if you're not sure where this should be done.) Place your frogs in the box or on the trash bag and spray them with the brown spray paint until they are completely covered. Then set the frogs aside to dry, about 20 minutes or until dry to the touch. If you painted your frogs outside and would like them to dry inside, just let them sit for 10–15 minutes, then bring them in to dry in an out-of-the-way location.

2. While the frogs are drying, use your scissors to cut the corkboard into 4 pentagon shapes about 6" across. You want them to be large enough to hold an average cup with enough room to glue on the frogs. Note: if your scissors won't cut the corkboard well, try cutting it with a craft knife. (Ask an adult for help if necessary.)

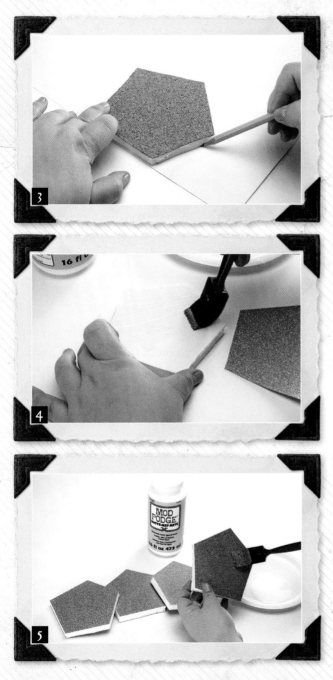

3. Use a pencil to trace the shapes of the pentagon onto the backside of the scrapbook paper, and use your scissors to cut the paper the exact sizes of your cork pentagons.

4. Use your foam paintbrush to paint a thin layer of Mod Podge onto the cork pentagons and place the pentagon scrapbook paper over them. Let this dry for 3–5 minutes or until dry to the touch.

5. Use your foam paintbrush to paint a light layer of Mod Podge on top of the paper for each coaster, covering it entirely. Allow this layer to dry for about 1 hour until dry to the touch, then apply another layer of Mod Podge. Repeat this same process one more time to ensure a good seal on the paper and let it dry to the touch once more.

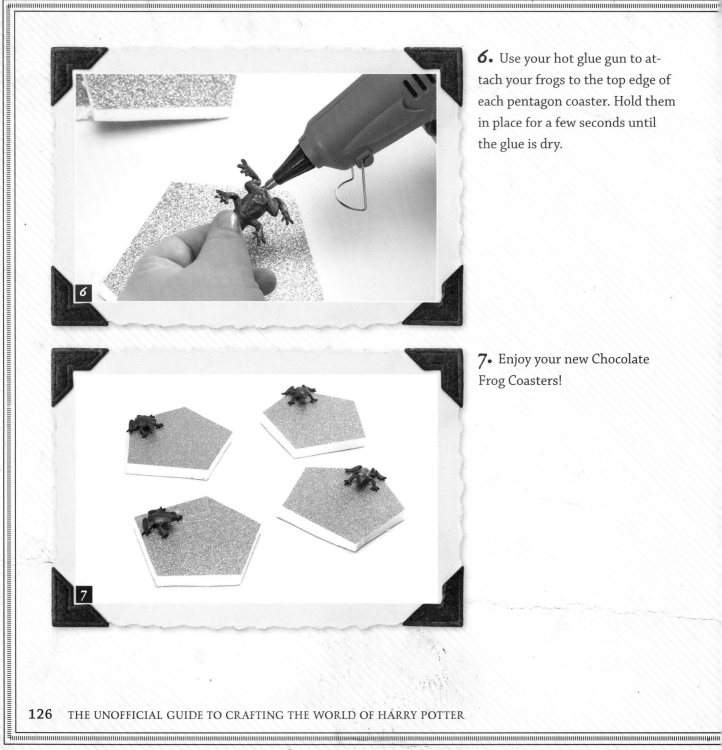

6. Use your hot glue gun to attach your frogs to the top edge of each pentagon coaster. Hold them in place for a few seconds until the glue is dry.

7. Enjoy your new Chocolate Frog Coasters!

TRANSFIGURATION TIPS

Print out pictures of your favorite wizards, glue them to the top of your coasters, and you will have Chocolate Frog Trading Coasters!

POTIONS ORNAMENTS

(by Dayna Abraham from *Lemon Lime Adventures* blog at *http://lemonlimeadventures.com*)

Harry had to spend every Christmas at Hogwarts, and with these Potions Ornaments, you can bring a little bit of Hogwarts to your house at Christmastime, too. These are a fun start to a totally Potter-themed tree! If you don't have a tree, or want to use these year-round, you can even hang them from your ceiling with a string!

WHAT YOU NEED:

To Begin

4 (83 mm) plastic globe ornaments

2 cups warm water

Polyjuice Potion Ornament

1 (10.5 ml) green glitter glue pen

1 tablespoon green glitter

2 drops green liquid food coloring

Felix Felicis Ornament

1 (10.5 ml) gold glitter glue pen

1 tablespoon gold glitter

2 drops yellow liquid food coloring

Veritaserum Ornament

1 (10.5 ml) white glitter glue pen

1 tablespoon white glitter

Amortentia Ornament

1 (10.5 ml) pink glitter glue pen

1 tablespoon pink glitter

2 drops pink liquid food coloring

To Complete

4 paper towels

Hot glue gun and glue

1 thin permanent black marker

HOW TO MAKE IT:

1. To Begin: Pop the top off of one plastic ornament and fill it about ½ full with warm water. Follow the steps for each individual ornament.

2. For Polyjuice Potion Ornament: Add the contents of your green glitter glue pen, your green glitter, and 2 drops of the green color dye to the water-filled ornament.

3. **For Felix Felicis Ornament:** Add the contents of your gold glitter glue pen, your gold glitter, and 2 drops of the yellow color dye to another water-filled ornament.

4. **For Veritaserum Ornament:** Add the contents of your white glitter glue pen and your white glitter to another water-filled ornament.

5. **For Amortentia Ornament:** Add the contents of your pink glitter glue pen, your pink glitter, and 2 drops of the pink color dye to the last water-filled ornament.

6. **To Complete:** Once the ingredients have been added to the water-filled ornament, cover the top of the ornament with a paper towel and shake until the ingredients are well mixed.

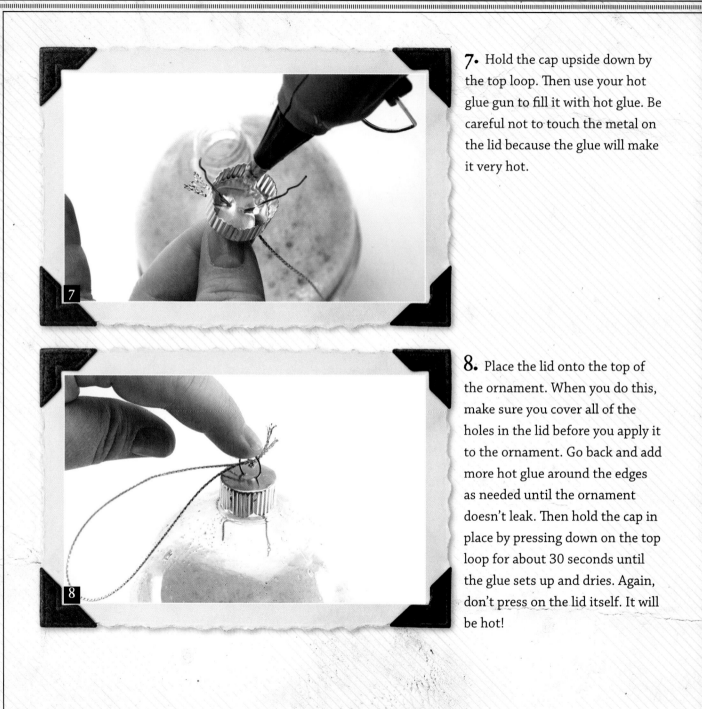

7. Hold the cap upside down by the top loop. Then use your hot glue gun to fill it with hot glue. Be careful not to touch the metal on the lid because the glue will make it very hot.

8. Place the lid onto the top of the ornament. When you do this, make sure you cover all of the holes in the lid before you apply it to the ornament. Go back and add more hot glue around the edges as needed until the ornament doesn't leak. Then hold the cap in place by pressing down on the top loop for about 30 seconds until the glue sets up and dries. Again, don't press on the lid itself. It will be hot!

9. Use your black permanent marker to write the name of your potion on the ornament.

10. A few seconds later, once the marker is dry to the touch, take your Potions Ornaments and hang them on your tree.

TRANSFIGURATION TIPS

Make these ornaments one at a time, because when you take off the top, you won't have anywhere to put them down once they are full of water.

HONEYDUKES COOKIE JAR

This cookie jar is one of my favorite things in my kitchen. And only the most ardent of fans would even know it was Harry Potter related. You don't have to write "COOKIES" on your jar either; you could write "CANDY," "SUGAR," "FLOUR," or even "HONEYDUKES" if you're a total purist. I won't be mad. So mix up a batch of butterbeer cookies and keep them in this adorable Honeydukes Cookie Jar!

WHAT YOU NEED:

1 (roughly ½ gallon) glass jar with a lid (You can find these in the housewares section of any craft store or department store.)

1 green and 1 pink oil paint pen (These are designed to write on ceramic and glass, and they won't chip off as easy as regular paint pens.)

HOW TO MAKE IT:

1. Use your pink paint pen to draw a pink diamond on the side of your jar about 5" across, large enough to write the word "COOKIES" in. Make the border about ½" thick but don't color inside of it.

2. Set the cookie jar aside for about 30 minutes until the diamond is dry to the touch.

3. Next, use your green paint pen to write "COOKIES" in all caps inside of the diamond. When you are writing, start with the *K* in the middle and work your way out, alternating each side so your word will be evenly spaced.

4. Set your jar aside to dry for 20–30 minutes, and when it's dry to the touch, your Honeydukes Cookie Jar is ready for your kitchen counter!

HALLECAKE SAYS

My favorite project in this
chapter is the Honeydukes
Cookie Jar. I always steal treats
from it . . . don't let my
mom know!

FREE DOBBY LAUNDRY HAMPER

You know what Dobby needs? Clothes. I always loved the fact that even though wizards had house-elves to do all their bidding, they had to deal with all their own wash or their elves would be free. Dobby is one of my favorite characters, and that's why I love how this laundry hamper assures all house-elves are free! This Free Dobby Laundry Hamper is a fun way to store your dirty clothes in your room.

WHAT YOU NEED:

1 (6" × 6") blank wooden sign

Black permanent marker

Fabric glue

Old sock

1 (14" × 14" × 23") cloth laundry hamper

HOW TO MAKE IT:

1. On your wooden sign, use your black marker to write "Free Dobby" with your nondominant hand. This will make it look like a house-elf who doesn't have very much practice writing actually wrote it.

2. Once your sign is dry, use your fabric glue to attach the old sock to the edge of the sign in the upper right-hand corner.

3. Lay your hamper down on its side and glue the wooden sign to the front of the laundry hamper at the top.

4. Set your hamper aside to dry for a couple of hours before using. Now you have a super-fun way to keep your dirty clothes off the floor!

HALLECAKE SAYS

Dobby! You were a free elf! <sobs>

CHAPTER 5

THE COMMON ROOM: CRAFTS FOR YOUR ROOM

The common room is *the* place to be if you are hanging out with your friends at Hogwarts—and don't have an Invisibility Cloak to sneak out with—and all the projects in this chapter will make your room look totally Harry Potter-rific too!

All over my house you will find cute little nods to Harry Potter. It might be the Lumos/Nox Light Switch Cover or the Mad-Eye Moody Photo Frame, but no matter what room you're in, you know I am a fan. I like these crafts because they are easy enough for anyone to do but still look like they were professionally made! Oh, and the Floating Candle Night Lights are now an essential part of every slumber party at our house.

LUMOS/NOX LIGHT SWITCH COVER

This glow-in-the-dark Lumos/Nox Light Switch Cover is such a neat thing to add to your Harry Potter–themed bedroom. It's fun because it glows again and again. Lumos is a fun spell to light up the night, and Nox will shut all those lights off again, which is pretty much what a light switch does anyway, right? Remember, since we are using an X-Acto knife, you might want to get some help with an adult for that part.

WHAT YOU NEED:

1 (8½" × 11") sheet of printer paper with the words "LUMOS" and "NOX" printed on it (I let several line breaks in between the two words and used a 45 pt Times New Roman font.)

X-Acto knife

Scotch tape

2 (1") foam paintbrushes

Black acrylic paint

1 standard white light switch cover

Acrylic glow-in-the-dark paint (This paint is clear, but it will have a slight yellow tint. You can get it at the craft store.)

Cardboard box or trash bag

Clear spray protectant

HOW TO MAKE IT:

1. Use an X-Acto knife to cut out each letter individually from the paper to create a stencil. If you're not sure how to use the knife or can't safely do so, ask an adult for help.

2. Use your tape to secure the "Lumos" stencil at the top center of the light switch cover, then tape the "Nox" stencil on the bottom center of the light switch cover.

3. Use a foam paintbrush to paint the inside of the "Lumos" stencil with black paint until the inside of the stencil is completely covered in paint. Let this dry for about 10 seconds and pull your stencil off the cover. Then let it dry an additional 10–15 minutes until it's dry to the touch.

4. Use the other paintbrush and the glow-in-the-dark paint to paint the inside of the "Nox" stencil until the inside of the stencil is completely covered in paint. Let this dry for about 10 seconds and pull your stencil off the cover. Then, once this is complete, set the light switch cover aside to dry for about 1 hour until it is dry to the touch.

5. Set up a place to spray-paint your light switch cover by placing your cardboard box or trash bag on the floor or outside on the ground. (Ask an adult for help if you're not sure where this should be done.) Place your light switch cover in the box or on the trash bag and spray it with the clear spray protectant until it's completely covered. Then set the light switch cover aside to dry, about 2 hours or until dry to the touch. If you painted your light switch cover outside and would like it to dry inside, let it sit for 10–15 minutes until dry to the touch, then bring it inside to dry in an out-of-the-way location.

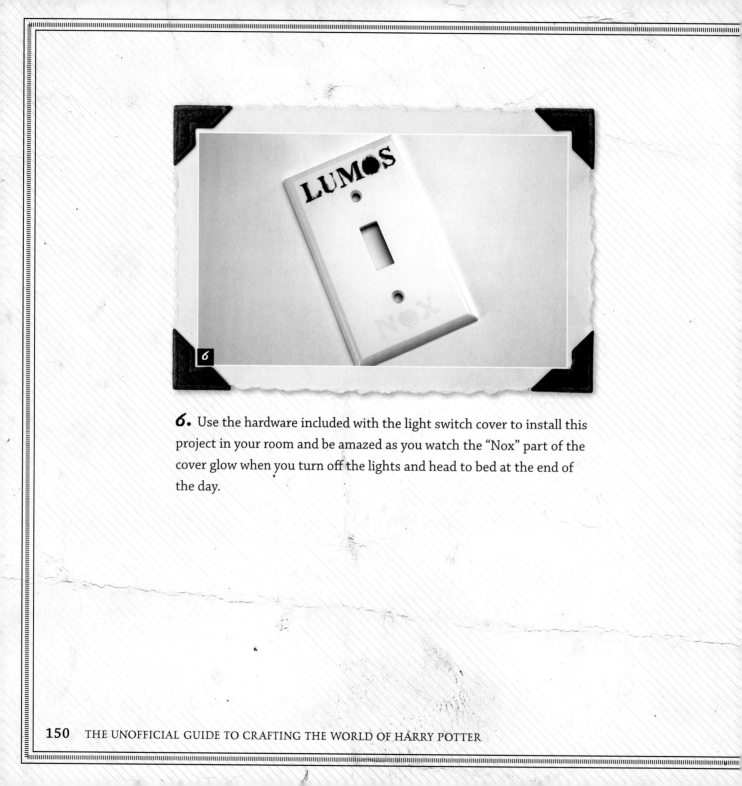

6. Use the hardware included with the light switch cover to install this project in your room and be amazed as you watch the "Nox" part of the cover glow when you turn off the lights and head to bed at the end of the day.

HALLECAKE SAYS

I'm in love with the Lumos/
Nox Light Switch Cover.
I feel just like I'm in the
Order of the Phoenix
using it!

FLOATING CANDLE NIGHT LIGHTS

Want to add a couple of floating night lights to your bedroom? These Floating Candle Night Lights are reminiscent of the floating candles that appear above the students' heads in the Great Hall and will make you feel like you are in a Great Hall of your very own!

WHAT YOU NEED:

3 toilet paper rolls

Hot glue gun and glue

3 battery-powered tea lights

1 (1") foam paintbrush

Off-white acrylic paint

1 sewing needle

3 (2') pieces of fishing line

3 thumbtacks

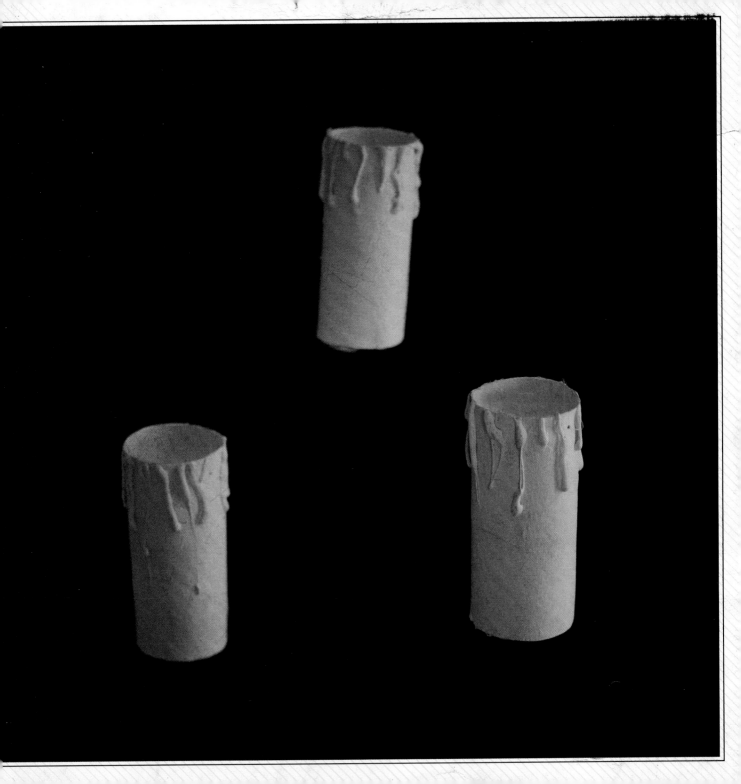

HOW TO MAKE IT:

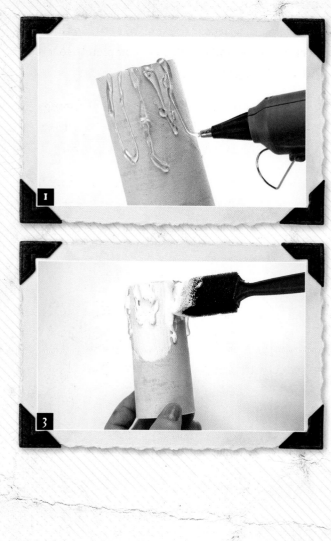

1. Stand the toilet paper rolls up vertically and take your hot glue gun and add glue around the top edges of each toilet paper roll, so it looks as if they are dripping wax. Set aside to dry for 2–3 minutes.

2. Drop 1 tea light into the bottom of each of your toilet paper rolls. Then use your hot glue gun to attach the tea lights to the edges of the rolls by adding the glue in between the roll and the edges of the tea lights. Let this dry for 2–3 minutes until the tea light will stay in the bottom of the candle when you hold it up.

3. Once the glue has hardened, use your foam paintbrush to paint the outside of your toilet paper rolls with the off-white acrylic paint and then set them upside down to dry for about 20 minutes.

4. If necessary, repeat the previous step so the toilet paper roll and the glue are completely covered in paint. Set aside to dry, about 20 minutes.

5. Using your needle, thread one piece of fishing line through the top of each of your candles, from one side to the other, and tie the ends together.

6. Finally, turn on your candles, then loop the wire under the thumbtack and tack them to the ceiling.

TRANSFIGURATION TIPS

You can cut the fishing wire in several different lengths if you want to give your candles a real floating feel!

MAD-EYE MOODY PHOTO FRAME

When you think of Mad-Eye Moody, you probably think of his ghastly mechanical eye. That eye is always watching, right? This frame may take a little while to assemble depending on how many eyes you use, but it looks really neat and you can make 2 or 3 of them to create a fun photo collage.

WHAT YOU NEED:

1 (4" × 6") wooden frame with glass

50–100 self-adhesive googly eyes in different sizes

1 (4" × 6") photo

HOW TO MAKE IT:

1. Pull the glass out of your frame and set it aside.

2. Peel the paper backings off of your googly eyes and adhere them to the frame, adding smaller ones in next to larger ones so that there aren't any gaps, sort of like a jigsaw puzzle.

3. Replace the glass and insert your photo into the frame.

4. Enjoy the coolest picture frame ever. Just be careful because the frame, just like Mad-Eye Moody, is watching you.

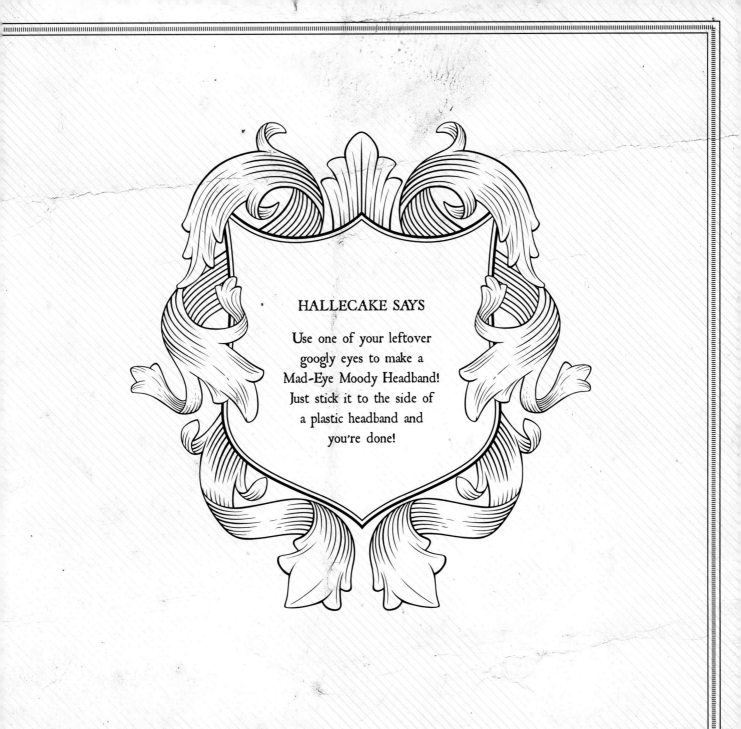

HALLECAKE SAYS

Use one of your leftover googly eyes to make a Mad-Eye Moody Headband! Just stick it to the side of a plastic headband and you're done!

WALL MIRROR OF ERISED

Unlike the true Mirror of Erised that Harry used to see his parents, and even the Sorcerer's Stone, this mirror won't show you everything you want to see, unless you just really like looking at your awesome self, but it will look awesome on just about any wall in your house. We did this to my daughter Halle's bathroom mirror and it is *amazing*! I love how the wall mirror can be hung up in a bedroom and used every day!

WHAT YOU NEED:

Painter's tape or masking tape, any width

Enough newspaper to cover the mirror part of your mirror

Scissors

1 mirror you can hang on the wall (I used a 12" × 12" mirror that has a thick, 3" frame, but you can use whatever size mirror you like as long as the frame is thick enough to decorate.)

1 bottle 3D fabric paint, any color

Cardboard box or trash bag

Silver spray paint

HOW TO MAKE IT:

1. Use your tape and newspaper to cover the reflective part of your mirror. You can use your scissors to cut the newspaper to size. Take your time doing this, because you don't want to get any paint on the shiny stuff.

2. Use your tube of fabric paint to write "Mirror of Erised" in fancy, cursive letters on the top part of the frame.

3. Now use the fabric paint to draw some fancy swirls on the sides and the bottom part of the mirror frame. Set this aside to dry overnight.

4. Set up a place to spray-paint your mirror by placing your cardboard box or trash bag on the floor or outside on the ground. (Ask an adult for help if you're not sure where this should be done.) Place your mirror in the box or on the trash bag and spray it with the silver spray paint until it's completely covered. Set the mirror aside to dry, about 2–3 hours or until dry to the touch. If you painted your mirror outside and would like it to dry inside, let it sit for 15 minutes until dry to the touch, then bring it inside to dry in an out-of-the-way location.

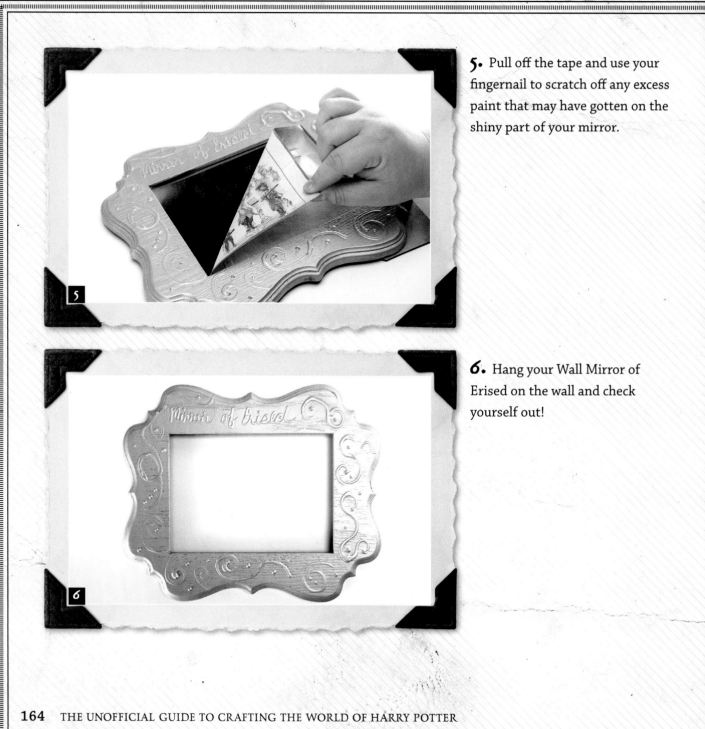

5. Pull off the tape and use your fingernail to scratch off any excess paint that may have gotten on the shiny part of your mirror.

6. Hang your Wall Mirror of Erised on the wall and check yourself out!

TRANSFIGURATION TIPS

If you want to go all out, do this on your bathroom mirror instead of just a small mirror you hang in your room.

CHAPTER 6

THE DARK FOREST: CRAFTS FOR THE GREAT OUTDOORS

Y̲ou remember the Dark Forest, right? It's the strictly off-limits place where Harry and Ron followed the trail of spiders to meet Aragog. While the crafts found in this chapter are for the outdoors, they are anything but forbidden—unless you don't believe in magic . . .

Maybe you have normal, boring Muggle neighbors that know nothing about the Potterverse and how much fun it is, or maybe you have crazy, awesome neighbors who love Harry Potter as much as you do. But how will you ever know if you don't place Nargles for the Yard on your lawn or add a Slytherin Snake Door Wreath to your door? And if you put the House Banners Doormat out in front of your house, it's always fun to see if guests notice the meaning behind the colors when they stop by—but only let them come inside for Chocolate Frogs if they're true fans!

SLYTHERIN SNAKE DOOR WREATH

I know you're out there, you Slytherins with your love of snakes and your gray moral compass. And this slimy, snake-covered door wreath isn't just fun to make; it's also fun to watch people freak out through the peephole when they realize what it is you have hanging on your front door!

WHAT YOU NEED:

Hot glue gun and glue

75–100 plastic snakes (I found a big bag of them in the toy section of a big-box store.)

1 (16") grapevine wreath (You can find blank wreaths with nothing on them at a craft store, or if you have an old wreath you don't like, you can just pull everything off of it and use that.)

Cardboard box or trash bag

Silver spray paint

HOW TO MAKE IT:

1. Use your hot glue gun to attach as many of the snakes as you can fit onto the wreath. You don't need to follow any sort of pattern or anything, just glue them on. You can put them on top of each other so they look like they are in a nest, or you can spread them out. Let this dry for 5 or so minutes until secure.

2. Set up a place to spray-paint your wreath by placing your cardboard box or trash bag on the floor or outside on the ground. (Ask an adult for help if you're not sure where this should be done.) Place your wreath in the box or on the trash bag and spray it with the silver spray paint until it's completely covered. Set the wreath aside to dry, about 2–3 hours or until dry to the touch. If you painted your wreath outside and would like it to dry inside, let it sit for 15 minutes, then bring it in to dry in an out-of-the-way location.

3. Hang your wreath on your door all year long, because that's how a true Slytherin would do it.

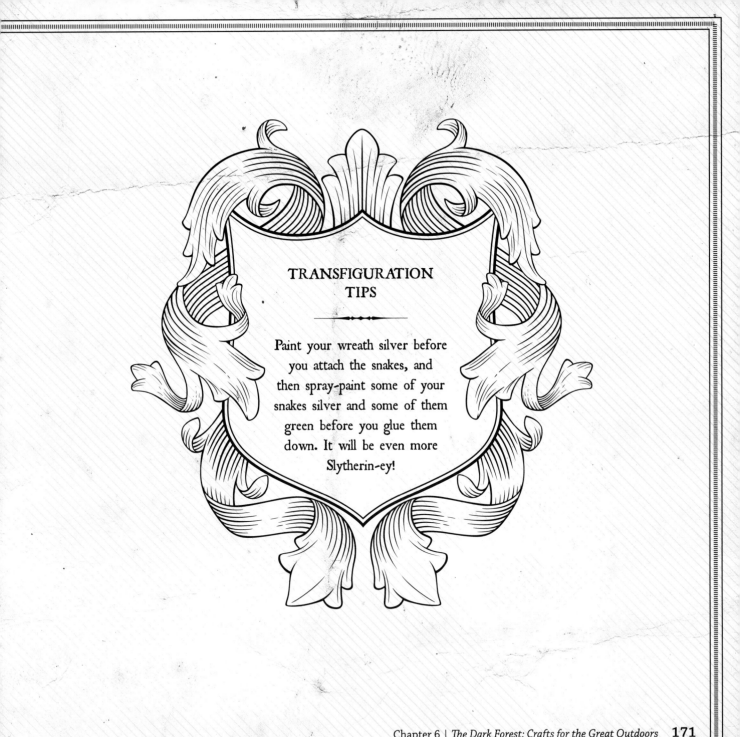

TRANSFIGURATION TIPS

Paint your wreath silver before you attach the snakes, and then spray-paint some of your snakes silver and some of them green before you glue them down. It will be even more Slytherin-ey!

NARGLES FOR THE YARD

Luna Lovegood swears Nargles exist and that they are constantly stealing things and causing mischief and mayhem right under everyone's nose, but the thing about Nargles is that nobody has ever actually seen them to know what they look like, which is what makes this project so fun! This project teaches you how to create little yard Nargles that will make it seem as though your whole yard is infested with these crazy creatures!

WHAT YOU NEED:

Elmer's Glue-All (It's important that you use Glue-All and not school glue, because school glue will just wash right off.)

1 paper plate

1 (1") foam paintbrush

10 small rocks, about 1" in diameter (You can buy these at any craft store, but you can also find them in the aquarium aisle at big stores, too.)

1 (4-ounce) jar of glitter (It doesn't matter what color; these are your Nargles so make them whatever color you want them to be!)

HOW TO MAKE IT:

1. Pour some glue out onto the side of your paper plate. Then, use your paintbrush to cover the top side of your rocks in glue.

2. Once your rocks are covered in glue, sprinkle the glitter onto them until the top side of the rocks are completely covered in glitter. Set your rocks aside to dry to the touch, about 15 minutes.

3. Once dry, flip over the rocks and repeat the process on the other side, covering them in both glue and glitter, then set your rocks aside to dry to the touch, about 15 minutes.

4. Repeat Steps 1–3 again so your rocks are super glittery.

5. Once dry, dip the rocks in the glue one last time to seal them so they will be weatherproof.

6. Set your rocks aside and let them dry really well, about 1 week. Then, take them outside and hide them in between tree branches, in your flower beds, behind your rain gutters, and even in the bushes. When the sun hits them just right, they will sparkle and make people take a second look. If they ask if you saw anything, you can shrug and say, "It's probably just the Nargles."

HALLECAKE SAYS

This project is my favorite one in this chapter. It makes me feel just as sane as Luna. Don't just stick these in your own yard; put them in your friends' yards, too. See how long it takes them to notice!

HOUSE BANNERS DOORMAT

This House Banners Doormat is pretty simple to make, but it is such a bold statement in front of your house, and it looks awesome. The four house crests are always on display throughout the movies and are mentioned throughout the books, and it's fun to bring them all together on one rug. One of the things I really love about it is that when it starts to look worn, you can just pull out your paint and fix it up again!

WHAT YOU NEED:

1 black permanent marker

Yardstick

1 (24" × 36") plain natural doormat

Scissors

2 (22" × 28") pieces of posterboard

Painter's tape or masking tape, any width

Red, green, blue, and yellow spray paint (red for Gryffindor, blue for Ravenclaw, yellow for Hufflepuff, and green for Slytherin)

Cardboard box or trash bag

HOW TO MAKE IT:

I. Use your yardstick to measure the mat width-wise. Divide the width by 2 and use your marker to mark this width with a small dash on the edge of the mat. Move your yardstick across the width of the mat marking the half point every few inches. This will create a straight line of dots across the center of your mat.

2. Now use your yardstick to measure the mat length-wise. Divide the length by 2 and use your marker to mark this length with a small dash on the edge of the mat. Move your yardstick across the length of the mat marking the half point every few inches. This will create a straight line of dots down the middle of your mat.

3. Line up your yardstick along the dash line running across the center of the mat and use the marker to draw a straight line along the yardstick. Then line up your yardstick along the dash line running down the middle of the mat and use the marker to draw a straight line along the yardstick. Now you have 4 equally sized boxes, 2 on top and 2 on bottom.

4. Place the tape on the outside edge of half of the vertical line and half of the horizontal line, to create a rectangular box on the doormat.

5. Set up a place to spray-paint your mat by placing your cardboard box or trash bag on the floor or outside on the ground. (Ask an adult for help if you're not sure where this should be done.) Place your mat in the box or on the trash bag.

6. Place the edge of one piece of posterboard along the tape running length-wise. Place the edge of other piece of poster board along the piece of tape running width-wise (this piece of posterboard will overlap the first piece of posterboard). One rectangle of the mat should be left exposed.

7. Spray your first color in the exposed rectangle on the mat and set the mat aside to dry, about 30 minutes or until dry to the touch. Once the mat is dry, remove the tape.

8. Add new tape to the two outside edges of another rectangle, then move the posterboard so it frames up this new, unpainted rectangle. Spray your second color in the exposed rectangle on the mat and set the mat aside to dry, about 30 minutes or until dry to the touch. Once the mat is dry, remove the tape.

9. Repeat the previous step until all the rectangles on the mat have been spray-painted with a different color.

IO. Set your House Banners Doormat aside to dry overnight. Then set it out in front of your house for all your guests to see.

TRANSFIGURATION TIPS

Instead of dividing this mat into
4 rectangles, try making it
with 4 diagonals or even
4 columns!

ACKNOWLEDGMENTS

My family puts up with a lot to live with a creative nerd like me. A special thanks goes out to my husband, the Ravenclaw, Kevin Gomes, for being so understanding when every empty surface of our house is covered in craft projects, and my beautiful Gryffindor daughter, Halle Harrington, who is always willing to craft with me, listen to my ideas, and call me out when I come up with an idea that is "like, totally dumb, Mom."

Katie Corcoran Lytle (such a total Ravenclaw), my editor, who took the words I wrote, unscrambled them, and made them so everyone else understood what I was trying to say. Kate Schafer Testerman (also a Ravenclaw) has been my agenting hero for more years than I care to admit, and it was so much fun to work with her on this project. Christine (Dumble)Dore (a Hufflepuff!) came up with the brilliant idea to write this book and plucked me out of a crowd to be the author, and for that I am forever grateful. And Holly Homer (who has to be a Gryffindor; she's the bravest woman I know)—what can I say about my friend, my confidant, and the only person I will ever go into business with. Without her freeing up my time so I could write, this book wouldn't exist.

A special thanks to my guest writers, and close friends. This book couldn't have been possible without Brittanie Pyper (also a Gryffindor), who spent countless hours helping me figure out how to make the perfect dementor tail, and came up with so many of these ideas. She really is my hero, and she will never ever realize it. Mary Duncanson (the only Slytherin I would ever hang out with), who was also there for me when I had a deadline that I thought was impossible to meet. She helped me find my words when I had none, and cheered me on when I wasn't sure I knew what I was doing!

Without these people, I'd probably be sitting in a bathtub eating cotton candy wondering why my life wasn't going anywhere, so I am super grateful for all of them.

INDEX